BREAKING POVERTY

How to eliminate obstacles and gain financial freedom on any salary

NATCOLE STASKIEWICZ

TO MY PARENTS

James and Debra for raising me to believe that
anything is possible.

TO MY HUSBAND

Michael for making everything possible.

TO MY KIDS

Amyia and Tighe, who inspire me to give you the
world.

TABLE OF CONTENTS

PREFACE

——— ✑ ———

Where do I begin? First, let me say there are no judgments here. We are human, and we are expected to make mistakes; However, what is most important is what we learn from those mistakes. I'm sharing with you the lessons I've learned that help me break free from a poverty mindset, and in return, I am growing more successful in life than I could have ever dreamed.

Through my lessons and my bonus material, you will gain insight on how you can overcome those obstacles that prevent you from breaking through that endless cycle of not making ends meet.

DREAMING

DREAMING

———— ◦⟋⟍◦ ————

A dream to have a nice career, home and wealth were all that it was at one point in my life, a dream. This may sound naïve, but I use to think that good situations would just happen to me because I am a good person. I used to think that If I weren't born into money, I would never have a lot of it. I had thoughts of never retiring wealthy unless I hit the lottery and that somehow my older self would make way for me to make things happen. When I was in my early twenties, "Adulting," as they would call it now, I had no idea of what to expect from this thing called "life." Truth be told, I am learning every day.

Growing up, I didn't have a lot compared to others. Notice, I said, "compared." My focus was on what others had. That somehow became of measurement of what I should obtain and become. Going back to when I was a teen, I looked at my friends that always seem to have designer clothes and named brand shoes, while I wore the generic clothing and was rocking them XJ900's and ProWings. If you don't know what those are. Don't worry; I am just showing how young I am.

Looking back, there was nothing wrong with them, but during that time, you didn't want to be caught wearing name branded Payless and Kmart shoes because belittling was in your future. The idea was It meant you were a nobody and you were broadcasting being broke. So, if you were going to wear branded shoes, Nike and KSwiss were the top brands during my childhood. Why am I going on about clothing and shoes, you may ask? Because this was the start of having the incorrect mindset for me. Paying more money just to wear a piece of clothing with a designer name seemed important at the time. My focus was not on the understanding that saving and spending wisely would allow me to afford more than the essential items. The pressure to keep up with the "in" crowd was always on.

I thought what mattered was how you were portrayed to the outside world. I focused more on material things and thought that If you were successful, you had to buy things in order, such as a house, a nice car among other objects. I constantly compared myself to others. Boy, did I still have some growing up to do?

There is nothing wrong with having those things, but most of my decisions were driven by an incorrect perception. So many people feel this way, so I thought this was normal, but It had to change.

How many times have you heard someone say, "If only I knew then what I know now, things would be different, or I would have made better or different choices"? Well, this is my gift to you. No matter what age you are now when you are reading this book, it does not matter. Prior choices that you later regret does not matter here. What we don't do here is worry about spilled milk. We make decisions based on what we know to date. I'm not making any excuses. I am just stating a fact. You must forgive yourself and move on.

My life was so complicated. I couldn't see another way of doing things. I always came up short financially, give into setbacks, misplace blame and allow distractions. I didn't think I could accomplish more because I didn't know exactly what that looked like. Everyone was trying to do the best they can with what they had. I just knew I wanted to do more than survive, and I did.

If you enjoy the struggle of not being able to make ends meet, then this book is not for you. It focuses on overcoming that and so much more. If you are that person that complains and won't change or refuse to put forth an effort to improve your situation, respect our differences and gift this book to someone who is ready. Following this journey that I am going to share with you has allowed me to reduce my monthly bills from $2500 to $800 a month and pay off $80,000 of debt in just under four years. I mean business here. My goal is to connect with individuals who feel they are stuck and have the means to change but simply don't know how.

Individuals who want to learn how to gain financial freedom, peace of mind and accomplish anything you set out to do, please read on.

A LIGHT PURSE IS A HEAVY CURSE

A LIGHT PURSE IS A HEAVY CURSE

Sooner or later, you will reach the point where you can't take it anymore. Before, I would take the money I made and spend my whole check. It wasn't the plan, as if I actually had a plan, it just sort of happened. I didn't feel I had enough to save, and if I did, something would come along and take it away. Even though I had an income, I always felt broke. I did not manage the money. Whenever I splurged on anything, I would often have that feeling you get in the pit of your stomach of trouble. The same feeling you got as a child when you've done something wrong, and you know there are repercussions at home. I felt that way because I knew there was a bill that I would no longer have enough money for since I couldn't resist the temptation to treat myself.

Always worrying if I would have enough to cover my bills and also not having enough to enjoy life was quite depressing. It was an everyday thing, and it weighed heavy on me. This was all I knew. I couldn't imagine there could be another way to manage finances. I thought the successful people were doing the same, but I was wrong. Some of my growth came from doing my own research, but most of all, I have to give credit to my one-on-one talks with God.

Before I proceed, I want to say don't miss out on a message that has the potential to be life-changing for you, just because you are not mentally there yet. I am sharing with you what turned things around for me. When I wasn't ready to listen when anyone mentioned "God," my ears turned off, and as a result, I missed out on many answers to my prayers. My life did not improve when I restricted myself. I know I'm preaching to the choir if you are a believer, but if you are not, then you only stand to gain from what I have to say. Just think about it. You already know the outcome of doing things your way. Try being open to another.

The more open I was to God, the more I heard him. It started out as a whisper. I couldn't distinguish if it were my own thoughts, but they gradually became more apparent. No, I was not going crazy. We have instincts and each of us have experienced situations where we have impulses to do and make certain decisions and can't explain why. When you can make the connection, and the result is you missed out on being involved in an accident or that choice allowed you to receive a promotion, and there was no other way you could have known that would be the outcome. I call that God. Now back to what I was saying…

I made promises to myself in hopes to improve my financial status. Such as, if I get a lump sum of money, I'll pay off whatever bills that were bothering me at the moment or if I hit the lottery big, I would pay it all off. It wasn't often that I was getting lumps sums of money, and you know how hard it is to hit the lottery big, so I didn't feel I would ever get ahead and be rid of all this debt. Despite not receiving a lump sum of money, I wasn't doing more with the stable income I had coming in. I had the mindset and behavior of not attempting to rid myself of my debt until one of the two promises were met.

I prayed more. "I need more money." Then all of a sudden, I heard God say, "Would you give your child more money if they were mismanaging it?" I was blown away. I had to really think about it. It was true. After I made those promises, I went through multiple jobs, but still I was no closer to freeing myself of the debt. In fact, I had accumulated more.

Then I thought deeper. With each job, I acquired I had an increase in salary. From the point of when the promise was made to the time I had this revelation, my income had increased by more than 75%. I couldn't believe I hadn't made the connection on my own. I had been hitting the lottery per se every time I got an increase. It may not have been all at once, but nevertheless I still got it. Yet, I still did not attempt to make good on my promise. I increased my lifestyle and added more reoccurring bills to the pile. In addition to that, I received a yearly tax refund, which is a form of a lump sum of money. I still did not do what I said with that. Instead, I was more focused on purchasing items that were put off throughout the year.

I was so disappointed with myself. Why would he bless me with more when I am not responsible and appreciative of what he has already given me? I cried. I start to think about how far he has brought me. Thankful that I was not where I was in the beginning, but I was still miserable. It was a pivotal moment in my life. That instant, although sad, also felt liberating. My eyes were opened, and everything appeared to be clearer. This was one mistake I won't dare repeat.

One of the good things about the world is the advancement of technology. I did not know exactly how to climb out of my mess and unlearn bad habits, but the number of resources available today left no excuse. I also made sure my circle consists of positive influences and people who would uplift and help me grow in the direction I needed. I really didn't care what others thought of me anymore or how I may portray myself to be. That kept me broke with the appearance of having it together on the outside. I wanted to be right on the inside too. I did not make time to entertain individuals who instead chose to place their own fears and restrictions on me. Unfortunately, if you grow up in an area or surround yourself with individuals who are less fortunate you will hear things like "You think you're better than them." because you are improving your life. Don't spend your energy trying to convince these people. If they feel that way, then that is their truth, and they need to address it head-on to change that. Overall, no one is better than anyone. We choose different paths, and we grow. You don't have to prove anything to anyone. If you are admiring what someone else has that you lack. Seek out how to change that instead of trying to bring the person down. Who in their right mind could ever blame a person for not wanting better? I want everyone to succeed, but the reality is you can't take everyone with you. If you are afraid; it's natural. I felt that too and I still do, any time I venture off past my comfort zone. Sometimes we can get scared to embark on a new path and take steps back, but I encourage you to press on. You will surprise yourself.

In doing my research, I learned the reason I was always fearful of something always coming along and taking any extra money I had was because I didn't budget. I wasn't really keeping up with the monthly expenses. Everything was in memory and not written down, so then I forgot about transactions and had gone through multiple periods where I over-drafted my account.

I can remember one time I was hit with seven overdraft fees at one time because I was off by $10. I had enough money to cover the six transactions and only one should have caused an overdraft, but do you know what the bank did? They took the highest transaction and paid it out highest to lowest. The highest transaction was enough to send me into the negative, so that resulted in seven fees instead of one. I still think that was bogus, but I won't start on that.

The bottom line is the Bank is in the business to make money and I made it easy for them to take advantage of me because I didn't do my part and budget. I couldn't blame anyone else and had to take responsibility for my part that I took in that instance.

I'm not going to sit here and say I never over-drafted my account again. I had struggled to keep a routine of budget and had sometimes fallen into old habits of forgetting to write everything down and that good ole automatic withdrawals got me again.

I had finally reached the point of being tired of giving away free money to the bank and stuck to a budget. I wrote down all my reoccurring bills every month. It helped me pinpoint where I was wasting money too. I felt more in control and was able to start a real plan of putting money aside for savings.

HAVING CAKE AND EATING IT TOO!

HAVING CAKE AND EATING IT TOO!

⸻ ❧ ⸻

Before I created the budget and list all my expenses, I had to be real with myself. I had to write down every single transaction. That included my routine trips to restaurants, clothing stores and coffee shops. I was amazed at how far I was living above my means. I didn't realize it until that moment that I never really sat down and did this calculation because I was afraid of what that number would look like. I was spending up to $1500 more than I had coming in. I was using credit cards to supplement the difference. I decided to go back and compare my expenses against each salary I had at the time and discovered despite my increases; I was still overspending. I knew this previously, but I didn't know exactly how much.

When I was making close to minimum wage, I was overspending by $300 every month. When I got my next increase, I was overspending by $500. That trend continued with every increase. How smart was that? I can only speculate that God was watching me doing this and saying, "I see that you were struggling and overspending $300 every month, so I blessed you to rid you of that shortage, and you did what?" I know. I know. All I can say is thank goodness he is a forgiving God and don't give up on you when you make repetitive mistakes.

When I finally created the budget, what came next was some real sacrifices. I started by only giving up **some** of my pleasurable visits. That helped to free up some money. Whatever I had remaining, I would divide it. I usually place some in savings and split the rest to pay down multiple credit cards. I still would have my guilty pleasures, but not as much. I thought I was doing something, but in actuality, I was diluting my efforts. That didn't become clear until "Murphy" happened. Do you know Murphy's Law? If it can go wrong, it will.

I had a sudden job loss, and I felt like I was left holding the bag. I still had credit card balances, car notes and student loans. Not to mention I had the responsibilities of a family, house, utilities, cable and any activities we would partake in to live comfortably. What was I going to do? I asked myself this over and over again. I thought I was on the right track, and now this. I asked God for help. With so much emotion, I was blurting out every "why" question I could think of. "Why does this always seem to happen to me? 'Why can't I get ahead?" "Why is this happening now that I'm doing so good?" While I was asking these questions, I suddenly started to feel bad that I was only looking to him for guidance when things were going wrong. I began to feel ashamed again.

I sat in my room quietly, and I was met with my own questions I felt compelled to answer.

"Why do this always seem to happen to me?"

Because I did not prepare for it.

"Why can't I get ahead?"

Because I won't allow it.

"Why is this happening now that I'm doing so good?"

Because I had to have my cake and eat it too.

I was doing this to myself! I felt like I reached another level of clarity. Yes, I made a budget, but I was only putting the bare minimum in savings. I did not cut out enough of my extra spending to make a big enough impact on what I was trying to do, which was to have a large enough savings and eliminate debt. Why did I feel like I was worthy of treating myself? I still was not sacrificing enough to make this goal attainable.

This might get too real for you. What I did next is a must. You don't have to like it, but I'm going to tell you it is the difference between those who are successful and those who wish they were.

NO PAIN NO GAIN

NO PAIN NO GAIN

―――――― ⤳ ――――――

W hen I became employed again, I went hard core. People around me thought I lost my mind. I re-examined my budget and practically cut out everything. I stopped using the charge cards; I canceled my streaming subscriptions, no more window shopping, no amazon, no restaurants unless the hubby was treating, no coffee shops, manicures, pedicures. Are you still with me? No new clothes, no trips, my hair was only professionally done once every four months. I became the coupon queen. I went from paying over $200 for 3 lines on a cell phone bill to $120 for 4 lines.

I was not playing. I had experienced no income for almost 5 months. During that time, I was unsure about my future, but the only thing that was certain was my debt. Unemployment was running out. We were doing okay for now, but I didn't know how long before it affected putting food on the table. I started thinking about how my car was going to get repossessed, how we could lose the house. We could lose everything because I wasn't responsible. My imagination ran wild.

I thought, "Okay, Lord, I'm ready to do it your way. Guide me; I'm ready to listen." I did my best to follow his word blindly. One of the things I learned from this journey is that you don't always have to connect the dots in order for a connection to exist. He is always working for you in the background, moving people, moving parts to prepare you for your blessing. It's not always meant for you to see the whole picture when you are taking steps.

I took that lesson to heart, and I had tunnel vision for this debt. It had to go, and since I eliminated so many expenses, I was now in the position to be able to start paying it down. Before I could get to that point, first I had to build up a starter emergency fund. In the beginning, "Murphy" was visiting often, and It was very discouraging. I chose to take a positive approach and remind myself that at least I had the funds to cover unexpected expenses. The emergency fund should not be used for events you failed to plan; In fact, I strongly advise you to keep it in a separate bank.

When I begin paying extra on the debt, do you know what happened? Money seemed to come out from out of nowhere. I'm talking about lump sums as well. There was more overtime available than usual at work. I received random refunds for the overpayments. How about that? I started brainstorming on what else I could do to help speed things along. I settled mostly on providing technical services to my clients and also network marketing. They both helped me considerably.

Then one by one, the debt started to disappear. I started with the smallest balances. It took too long and felt too disappointing when I was paying extra on multiple bills at once. Focusing on one at a time was easiest. When I started this journey, my debt was at $115,000. Due to some unforeseen medical bills, it had ballooned to $130,000.

That is a large number to take in and it can be easy to be intimidated by it. What I did is focus on $10,000 at a time. I don't look at the overall number too much. It is hard to convince yourself that you can pay off such an enormous amount. Especially when you are walking a new path you have never experienced before. Trust me just focus on a small amount at a time and create mini-goals. It will help you stick to it.

To break it down even further, once I received any income, I would take care of all my essential reoccurring bills, such as food and utilities. Can you guess what I did with the rest of it? That's right; I put everything remaining on the smallest debt. Even If I had received a check that had overtime hours, it would not matter. Every time I freed up cash, I would apply that and anything more I could find to the next commitment in line. After paying everything out of my main checking account, I would have a balance as low as fifteen cents remaining. Are you still here? Listen, I no longer live paycheck to paycheck because of this, so stay with me.

I was not super panicked because everything was paid, and I had funds set aside in case of something unexpected. I'm not going to lie and say it was easy. In the beginning, I fought with situations like not putting an extra item in the cart. It was hard to resist sales. I wanted so badly to only focus on building my savings. I didn't want to give it all away.

I constantly turned to God. "Please help! I think I'm about to give in.", "This is too hard!". Then I felt him say, "Don't worry about the money, I will give it back to you.", "Your savings will grow." Now, what I took from that was that because I made a commitment to these loans, I had the responsibility to pay them back. Once I am free from it, I will continue to be blessed and my savings will flourish. With that understanding, I tell myself every time I want to slip up, "The faster I can get them out of my pockets, the faster I can get my money back." Unless the item I want to purchase is being discontinued and will no longer be available EVER, there is no reason you can't wait to obtain the item until you have reached the goal."

If you think about it, it won't matter if it is on sale or not. You can afford it. Have you ever went shopping in a store and picked out a bunch of items without looking at a price tag? It can happen. Think about what is your worst-case scenario right now? If you lost your job today, what would you be forced to give up? Really think about it. If you haven't already, you will start to realize how vulnerable you are. If you don't do anything about it, you are in for a rude awakening.

My sacrifices and restrictions were only temporarily, and that's how I viewed it in order to get through. Why wait for your worst-case scenario to happen before you get things together and do what you need to do? Start with creating a budget. I did this every month before I was paid. I took all the time to go over all the hard decisions in determining how much extra was going to be applied that pay period. When the day came, I would just do what I wrote down. I couldn't sit there and think about it again, or I might talk myself out of it. I wouldn't wait for the due date either. If a bill were to become due within a certain pay period, I would just pay it all on that day. I was able to adapt the budget when odd objects came up. One month I may need to allocate funds to buy something for the kids, or I might need something for myself. I didn't have much of a life, and that was okay. I was tired of "faking fine." It was time to demystify the illusion.

When I hit my first goal, I hollered! I couldn't believe the first $10,000 was gone. I thought, "I can really do this!". Then I hit my next goal. You couldn't tell me anything. With each goal I met, I felt more confident and more secure. I was ready for any mishaps. I increasingly felt a sense of entitlement. I was doing so good; I begin to have thoughts again on how I earned certain rewards. It's funny because it was as if God interrupted me and said, "Don't get ahead of yourself now." I sat my butt down really quick. He put me in my place. I chuckled, but then I thought that I was thankful God had my back.

I hope you become fortunate enough to experience that feeling. To have a connection with God. To hear him. To feel him. It's quite remarkable and difficult to explain. I get so emotional just thinking about it. I had more lessons I had to overcome, and through it all he has stayed by my side.

What I want you to take away from this is it doesn't matter how much you start with, just start. I guarantee if you stay focused It won't be the amount you end up with. I went from being behind all the time and robbing Peter to pay to Paul to forgetting I got paid. Can you imagine that? I couldn't, and now that is my new normal.

It doesn't matter If all you have to begin with is $20 extra dollars. Start there and it will balloon up into more. You might be amazed to know that there are people with six-figure incomes that are also struggling. Debt impacts us all the same. It introduces the same risk without prejudice. There is no sense in allowing the debt to hang around until something unfortunate occurs. You will feel the weight of it and develop a sense of eagerness to get rid of it. At that moment, there will be nothing that you can do. Your income has stopped, and you need every penny you have to stay afloat. That's the realism you do not see when you misjudge and don't feel the rush to take care of this. Heaven forbid if you lose your health. We don't know what the future holds; that's why you need to do this for the best interest of yourself and take care of it while you still have the ability.

You need to rip the band-aid off. If it's too difficult to begin as hard core as I have, give yourself a little room. Before, I was spending a minimum of $50 on coffee and an embarrassing amount of $300 eating out a month. When I felt like I was going to cave in and splurge, I occasionally added it back into the budget and allow myself up to $15 on each category. You will have a newfound appreciation for those privileges and begin to view them as a treat again. It was minor, but It gave me something to look forward to. Making that adjustment alone freed up $320. What could you do with that?

I suggest you look through your bank statements. Go back at least six months and add up all your excess spending. Be prepared. You could be in for a shock; however, the good news is that it is your extra funds that you have to start applying towards your debt. As you continue to free up more cash, don't increase your lifestyle. Live as if you are really broke, which you technically are right now, but no need to focus on that because that is going to change.

This is not a time to be impatient. It took time for you to get into this situation it will take time for you to get out of it. That was a hard thing for me to cope with because I just wanted it over with. I played around with multiple budgets before I settled on one type. One was more of a gradual of extra payments, and the other was hardcore. I had the data prefilled for up to twelve months. Comparing the two, I noticed I could be out of debt four years earlier if I went hardcore.

Let me tell you, at the beginning; it hurt so bad to be putting all of that money towards something not tangible. I adopted the method of paying until it hurts. If it didn't hurt, it meant I was still too comfortable and was taking a gradual approach. I would pay; it would hurt, but I got it over with and then would look forward to the next month. If you decide to take that method, I can tell you the hurt feeling will go away. It will become ordinary to drop large dollar amounts to reach the goal much faster. Keep in mind that money will continue to gravitate towards you and will take your journey to another level.

If you haven't figured it out yet, it is crucial that you create a budget. What I found that worked best for me was to base my budget around each pay period. It included my anticipated paycheck amount and helped determine when each of the listed bills was due. I also recorded my emergencies. That served as an additional reminder and motivation while moving along to hit my milestones.

For instance, I may have a target to pay down $1000

by a certain time and may have missed a goal; however, when I check to see if I encountered any emergencies during that time, I find that I would have made or exceeded my goal. When you encounter this, just say to yourself. "Although the goal was not met, I am happy not only did I have the funds to cover the expense, but that I am still making progress and reducing my debt." I know you'd rather have it and not want to spend it versus needing money and not having it. The sooner it's gone, the less likely you will be left holding the bag.

If you are not happy with your salary, explore what you can do to change it. Work more hours, change jobs, advance your degree and get your certifications. If you have a special skill set look into freelancing. Create multiple streams of income. You can even sell Avon; I did and still do. No job is beneath you.

The mindset is so critical in your success. You will have to do as I have and combat the old way of thinking throughout this process. That little voice that says, "You have plenty of time to produce more funds." is false.

SETBACKS

SETBACKS

———— ⟷ ————

I had to recondition my mind. Those old habits continued creeping up, but it was nothing I couldn't fight to change. How you choose to perceive and react to circumstances affects everything around you. Once I realized that it was a game changer for me.

During the time I was sacrificing, it felt like everyone else was spending. I fought the habit of admiring the fact others seem to be able to live the life they want, while I was feeling deprived. They were going on trips and they were buying nice cars and gadgets. It seemed like everything I wanted at the time was in my face. I experienced occasions where I felt like I was missing out, but then I had to remind myself why I started this. I had to keep telling myself, "I got to do something different." "I can't continue to do the same thing and expect different results."

If you told me years ago that when I started out by applying an extra $50 a month would one day allow me to pay cash for whatever I want. I probably wouldn't have believed you, but that is exactly what happened! I kept my eyes on the prize and won it!

When I paid off my car, the old me would have signed up for another car note. Instead, I resisted the temptation, and $400 went back into my pocket. My income continued to increase, and I perceived debt as a liability. It made me vulnerable and threatened my family's livelihood. Even though I was able to do some things for them, I wanted to do more. I never want to worry about money again.

I used cash envelopes to help me budget expenses like food, clothing, and gas. I had sinking funds for things like clothing and back to school shopping for the kids, a veterinarian for our dog, Christmas and birthday fund. Although at the beginning the birthday fund had been cut out, I gradually added it back. For those of you that are not familiar with sinking funds, it has a constant cycle of being built up and depleted. I use these to save up for yearly occasions, and I use the cash envelopes to control the allotted cash per category per pay period. Once the envelope was empty, I spent no more in that category until I was paid again and can refill it.

I maintained focus and did not let temporary setbacks undo all the hard work I've done. I take a positive approach to everything because it can always be worse.

If I experience negativity, I always think about what my contributions are to avoid escalation or a recurrence. If I never seem to have enough for what I want to do, why is that? I ask myself, what is it I could be doing better to make this an untrue statement. I apply this in all areas of my life, and I recommend that you do the same.

Sorry to say there are no short cuts. Some people absolutely refuse to delay instant gratification, and that very thing is their downfall. Remember, it's only temporary. Surprisingly, I found when I reached the point of being able to buy the things I once couldn't resist; I didn't want them. Well, I did want them, but I didn't feel like I needed to get those things. It turns out that I only wanted them because I thought I could never have it. Now that I have choices, there was no feeling of urgency to obtain it.

When I messed up, I started again and again, never stopping. I did not dwell. I understood that I am an imperfect human. I am expected to stumble and fall. Any mistakes I made up to that point, and thereafter I considered to be a paid lesson.

Change your view not to compare yourself to others while you are on the journey to debt freedom. I guarantee you that some individuals are secretly wishing they had the discipline to do the same. So many people admired me but lacked the will power. They all had something in common, though. They each expressed how they thought it was unattainable for them to join me, but they were incorrect. It is simply a mind thing. If the doctor called you in the office today and said, "The debt you have will kill you unless you pay it all off within six months." I bet you every last one of those people will find a creative way to do it. It's that same drive you have when trying to cover a bill to avoid shut off. It's the same drive you have when there is an item you oh-so desire and cannot afford, yet you somehow find a way. Put a positive spin on your methods. Change your mindset to focus on eliminating the debt so that you can enjoy those things instead of it holding you back. If you don't think that your debt isn't holding you back, then you are living in a misconception. I can't say that enough.

Find you a support group that is following the same path and interest; otherwise, you will have a bunch of broke people in your ear giving you unsolicited advice on what you should be doing and how you're doing it wrong. You must stay away from the C.O.B.B. I call them the Circle of Broke Bitches. You might be thinking, "I'm broke. Is she talking about me?" But I'm not talking about your typical broke person. Most people mean well, but just do not understand, but these select individuals are your haters. They don't support you. They are rooting for you, but in secret, it's to fail. I want you to succeed and surround yourself around people who tell you that you can instead of those who sing, "Let me count the ways you can't."

I want you to get fed up and get fired up! Don't get discouraged by how much time it may take. That time is going to pass anyway. The question is, do you want to be broke or have it made by then? You can apply this logic in any part of your life as well! When I'm dieting. I want to eat the cake, but I got to decide am I going to eat that piece of cake while I'm disgusted with myself or while I'm healthy and have reached my goal with no regrets? I'm getting off topic, but you can see how you can apply all these methods to multiple areas of your life.

Start to anticipate what is within your control to minimize setbacks. For example, my current vehicle is ten years old and has over 200,000 miles on it. I know it will likely be sooner rather than later that I am faced with the decision to repair or replace. It would be wise to start a sinking fund or dedicate an emergency fund for **when** not **If** this happens. The old me would have known this as well, but instead, I would be hoping that it didn't happen until I was actually ready. Meanwhile, I wouldn't be saving anything for when that day comes, so I would actually never be ready. This is not how you get ahead. When there is a temporary calmness in your storm, you have to act now to turn things around. Get out of denial and start planning.

CONCLUSION

CONCLUSION

So now you have a choice to make. How bad do you want financial freedom? How bad do you want to see your dreams manifest? You can hold on to your money, continuously letting it pile, afraid to pay anything off because of some unknown emergency that may happen. You will find yourself still feeling uneasy because you still owe a lot of debt. Yes, you can fool yourself for a short period of time, but all it takes is one small mishap to poke holes in your strategy.

You can sit there and think of every reason why you can't (won't) do it, but it will not change the fact that you still remain exposed. You can't escape the characteristics it takes to become financially successful. Your best weapon against setbacks is to always nurture the right mindset and a good plan. I am hoping that you can benefit from the insight of my unfortunate highlights and my shared conversations with God. You are not stuck, and if you are, you can certainly make yourself unstuck. I plead with you not to place this responsibility on your older self. If you could go back in time and talk to yourself from ten or twenty or so years ago, what would that conversation look like? I will tell you it won't get much better when you get older if you haven't made any good moves towards a solid future.

Stop looking for a quick fix and put in the work on yourself. You are worth it! Take your focus away from the "in" crowd because most if not all of them are broke. What's worse is a lot of them don't even realize it. You have to emulate the right people that have the same goals as you and are achieving results. They each have identifiable traits. One side spends more on items that go up in value, and the other spends more on items that go down. Which side do you prefer to be on? You can't make it big with a broke mentality.

Just start, what do you have to lose? A lot, actually if you are not able to save right now. I'm not trying to be funny, just trying to wake you up before you are backed into a corner. As you move along in your journey, I would like to recommend Dave Ramsey as another great resource. His methods really helped me out tremendously and can provide you with an added push in the right direction. I hope that having insight on how I combated these emotional obstacles combined with the knowledge of how to defeat debt, motivates you to change your life. Please proceed on to the "Diversions and Disregarded Obstacles and the "Exercises" section. It can also help you along the way. I wish you the best of luck on your way to debt freedom.

DIVERSIONS AND DISREGARDED OBSTACLES

DIVERSIONS AND DISREGARDED OBSTACLES

Distractions

T here are many that I could discuss, but I would like to share with you a few other hurdles that I had to overcome that played a key role and may be an issue for you. The first one being distractions. It serves as a level of procrastination during your journey. You must learn to identify these and overcome them as well. It will remain a constant battle, but as long as you stay conscious of what's going on you can redirect yourself. I'm no exception to this. I just watched a few YouTube videos before typing this sentence.

The intention was to seek out ideas and motivation but prolonged, it can develop into something else. As what was supposed to be for fifteen minutes turned into an hour, God brought to my attention that I was being distracted by others success. I felt an internal nudge. "They did what they were supposed to do. Now what are you doing?" As always, he was correct. Again, I thought about what was happening. The people I was watching were tasked with creating the content, recording the video, then uploading it so that the viewers can see. They each successfully completed that and can now work on their next move to complete their goal. Meanwhile, I am sitting here being consumed by video after video when I have a target to reach as well.

I share this to say, use time limits whether you are in a research phase, looking for motivation, tools or more. If I didn't reach the point of managing my time, I could have been distracted by all my time going towards watching videos on how to do something instead of actually doing it. All your time could go on researching how to gain that financial freedom and less time on putting in the work. Discouragement can easily settle in, and before you know it, you could talk yourself out of it before you even started.

Because I stayed focused on my task, I was able to enjoy things like taking my whole family to California to see my grandfather, whom I hadn't seen since I was ten years old. He met my husband and kids for the first time. We spent multiple days at Universal Studios and appreciated other activities. We were able to purchase souvenirs. We ate plenty of overpriced food. It was expensive, and we spared no expense, but you know what? We thoroughly enjoy ourselves. What was even better is there was no sick feeling in the pit of my stomach. All my bills were paid with plenty of money left over. It is such a beautiful peace of mind. I want you to experience this. Maintain focus so that you will always be in the best possible position you can be for any scenario. When covid-19 hit, our primary worry outside of the obvious was toilet paper. Not many people could say that. I certainly couldn't once upon a time.

People

Unfortunately, another obstacle you will need to learn to overcome is people. Normally, they are not really a hurdle but, if you let them interfere with your money they can be. I also feel compelled to mention that no one can block your blessings either. Giving people too much power and allowing them to become a barrier, I can't tell you how many times I have seen others fall victim to this. They are so distracted by the wrong thing that they completely miss what's occurring.

While moving up in the corporate world, I am confronted with all sorts of people and have to deal with their mixed personalities, despite my having the best intentions to build good solid relationships. I encountered individuals that do not have my best interest at heart. Some will try to sabotage your progress. It is not your job to retaliate. Never let someone cause you to break out of your character, or it will result in you missing your blessing. If you change who you are because you have dealt with individuals who were not worthy of what you have to offer, well then, you're not the same person anymore. Your interactions change, and so your approach and the people you encounter going forward will change, and usually, it's not for the better. If you're like me, I wear my heart on my sleeves, and even though you know people can be cruel, it hurts to receive that type of negativity when you don't put that kind of energy out there.

I asked God to help me through this because it was affecting my ability to continue stable work environments to increase my income. I heard his reply, "Are you surprised?" and "Do they do this to anyone else?" I smiled, thinking to myself these were great points. Those people usually do behave the same manner to everyone, and No, I was not surprised. I keep that in mind and take no offense if the person that is doing the wrongdoing is staying true to their character. I am reminded I am not exempt. This has helped my sanity and kept me at a level head to minimize letting people interfere with my income or any other aspect of my life. I learned a long time ago that in time they would receive repercussions for their actions. I just ask the Lord sometimes to allow me to witness it.

You can't worry about who or what you can't control. Continue being who you are, improve yourself for the better, so when that opportunity comes along you will be in the right head space to receive it. There are going to be all kinds of people that you think can control your circumstances, and It may be true to some extent. On paper, you have a boss that controls the hiring and firing at a company, or there could be opportunities you would like to participate in, but it hangs on a referral from a person. They both have influences, but neither of them has the final say, and that's where my God comes in.

How many times did you encounter a situation where you thought the outcome was unfortunate in real-time but actually worked out in your favor? I want you to keep that in mind at all times. Especially if you're the type of person that can easily quit a job with a good income because of a person. Keep pushing on, and don't let people interfere with your goals. If you don't get an opportunity with one person, you will get it with someone else. Now "I have spoken.", as the Mandalorian's Kuiil would say it.

Teamwork makes the dream work

Lastly, but certainly, not least, you have to overcome "you." In addressing obstacles, you had to know I couldn't leave you out. You get in your own way too often. Letting fear rule your decisions. Placing all your energy into someone else's dreams and leaving next to none for your own. Fighting yourself on every turn to make the right financial decisions because of the emotions you feel.

You need to become one with yourself, a team. Whether that means one with God or if you're not a religious person and it just means more Intune with yourself. I personally don't feel I could have done any of this without God, but that is my belief.

I encourage you to go for what you want, no matter how impossible it may seem. Anything worth having requires some level of sacrifice. You can make this sacrifice now so that you can freely be who you are with peace of mind. What is it that you enjoy doing or would like to try? Do you like to go all out for events or would like to plan a trip and not worry about having little to no spending money? I don't like limitations. Do you?

Turn off your autopilot and ignore your emotions for right now. You need to venture off into the unknown, past your comfort zone, to get where you need to be. Don't overcomplicate this. I kept this book simple because I want you to do the same. If your emotions are conflicting with the goal, leave them at the door. I know easier said than done, but I know you can do it.

Feel that confidence. You have firsthand witnessed yourself in action when the drive to get what you want is present. It is there because you believe in the possibility. Believe that you can live a life without financial worry.

I will leave you with one final example that shows you how things can work when you get out of your way. I know a person that has a business goal that would require her to overcome public speaking. She seeks guidance from God as well to help her through her journey. There was an opportunity from the woman's small business administration that came across her path to potentially receive funds when hosting a webinar. The opportunity didn't present itself in a way she would have liked. She had less time constraints and didn't really feel she could meet the requested requirements in time. She instead passed the information along to others that could benefit from it.

Fast-forwarding to almost two weeks later, there was a requirement to host an international webinar at her place of employment. Everything she had to do to prepare would have met the requirements. She could have qualified for the cash. What was put off had to be done anyway, and she did a great job. There was no way for her to know that was around the corner. If she had blindly followed, she would have been in a better position to receive the experience with the added bonus of funds.

We all have visions of what the path to our journey should look like but be reminded we don't have the final say. The distance between point A to point B is not a straight line. This is what the Lord has made clear to me, and I hope it registers with you. "Don't worry about how I will get you there. Just know that I will get you there. You asked for guidance and I present the opportunities for you to take advantage of, not to question. My plan for you is at the forefront, which may appear to you as the background. I'm doing all the hard work. Don't worry about what it looks like. All will be revealed in hindsight."

Final Words of Encouragement...

Delaying instant gratification is not the end of the world. Change that inner narrative that you tell yourself. Say, "I'm restricting myself now, so that later I will have no limits." I hope you know as long as your still sucking air, it's not too late. God told me so and he hasn't steered me wrong yet.

Make sure you are mindful of temptations and be aware of your triggers. One of mine is purchasing technology, so when I find myself on the fifth unboxing video, I know I'm headed for trouble. You know how you operate, so try to avoid invitations that encourage overspending.

Don't complicate this. Keep it simple. Create a plan that includes anticipating setbacks for what is in your control. Fight those feelings of impatience along with any other traits that threaten this blissful future. Go ahead and form a budget so you can see how you can save your money for emergencies and eliminate debt. Once they're gone, your cash will stack so fast. Then you will be free to invest, which will take your journey out of this stratosphere. You will be able to make money while you sleep.

Don't listen to that little voice that encourages you to not follow through or procrastinate. Surround yourself with positive voices. If you have a special talent or message to share that could benefit someone else and resort to an increase in funds, don't discount it because it comes naturally to you. This is so critical.

I could have easily not written this book because of the fact that some people may already be aware of these strategies, but I know it's not enough to know what to do. You got to want it bad enough and believe in it too. My experiences are unique to me; I chose to share my journey in hopes of helping another. Because there was a time, I did not know how to get on the right track with money. To this day, I still can't fathom how much my life has changed just from making these key changes. I couldn't keep this to myself verbally, but I wrestled with putting pen to paper. I had been validated over and over again when I shared my outlook with others and watched them break barriers on their progress. I decided not to listen to that little voice. As a result, another stream of income has been created, and most of all, I get to help you. So shut that negative talk down. You have no idea of what opportunities will be birthed from taking chances. There are truly no limits to what you can do once you put your mind to it. Good luck!

BONUS EXERCISES

BONUS EXERCISES

Exercise 1 (Pen to Paper)

I would like you first to get out a piece of paper and write down the answers to the following questions.

1. Where would you like to see yourself financially in the next ten years?

2. What steps are you **currently** taking to make that possible in the future?

3. Are you dreaming or are you taking action towards your goals? What are your goals?

4. What do you feel is holding you back or could hold you back from achieving this goal? How can you minimize or remove this risk?

5. How much debt do you currently have? Student loans? Personal loans? Etc.

6. What steps are you **willing** to take to make this future possible?

Exercise 2 (Brain Dump)

1. Write down everything that you're spending. Be sure to include both essential and excess purchases.

2. Create a similar chart below and place each item in the proper category.

Needs vs Wants vs Waste (Monthly Chart)

Needs	Cost	Wants	Cost	Waste	Cost
Mortgage/ Rent	$900	Cable/Internet	$300	Restaurant Coffee	$30
Groceries	$800	Netflix	16	Cigarettes	$140
Total:	$1,700	Total:	$316	Total:	$170

Sample Chart

Needs category:

Although these are required items, you can still look into how you can reduce any of these expenses. Such as you can relocate or share rent with a roommate. For groceries you can purchase less or use coupons.

Exercise 2 continued.

Wants category:

These are desires that you enjoy allowing you to live comfortably. See what you can eliminate temporary. Remember no pain no gain!

Waste category

These bring you pleasure but no real value to your life. Which items can be removed from here?

Uh-huh! So, you do have extra money. What are you going to change?

Exercise 3 (Beast Mode)

Step 1. Commit to which items you will reduce or eliminate to free up cash.

Step 2. How long do you think it will take for you to pay off the debt? Write it down.

Step 3. If you got more aggressive, would that date change? If yes, write down the new date.

Step 4. Establish how much you want your starter emergency fund to be. (Depending on current salary, my suggestion is $500, $1,000 or $1,500)

Step 5. List your loan balances in order from lowest to highest.

Step 6. Create your budget

Step 7. Apply any extra money towards your emergency fund goal until met. (Do not move on until complete)

Step 8. Apply any extra money towards the lowest loan balance and pay the minimum amount to the remaining debt.

Step 9. Repeat step 8 until all debt is paid off.

Step 10. Fully fund your emergency fund

Step 11. Enjoy your money, Invest, take trips, remain smart with your money, let it grow.

Please visit NStaskiewicz.com for upcoming books and resources.